EMBRACE YOUR EMOTIONS

WORKBOOK

SHERESE SHY-HOLMES

CONTENTS

CHAPTER

1

I GOT A BIG EGO

We're all aware of our primal desires of the id and how we should curb them, but I want to encourage you to take a look at the superego too. We have the task, as we go through adulthood, to understand how the id impacts our decisions and to examine our superego. In addition, we need to determine where our inner critic is coming from and identify those limiting beliefs that keep us playing small in life. Here are some questions to work through:

1. Think about the id and how it's manifested in your decisions? Do you make impulsive decisions? If so, how has that affected you?

2. Since we are constantly moving away from pain or closer to pleasure, in what ways can you identify this principle operating in your life now (career, family, romantic relationships etc.)?

3. Growing up, who were the important influences that had a hand in developing your superego (ex: parents, caregivers, teachers, coaches etc.)?

4. What role has culture played in crafting your superego?

5. Which one of these limiting beliefs resonates with you?

    a. I am not worthy.

    b. I am not _____ enough (insert good, skinny, smart, rich, pretty etc.).

    c. I do not deserve the _____ (promotion, house, career etc.).

    d. I am unable to be loved or I am unlovable as I am.

    e. I don't have enough _____ (support, money, time, experience etc.).

6. Now, let's get specific. What kind of other limiting beliefs have you told yourself in areas like relationships, money, career, health etc.?

7. How are these limiting beliefs holding you back, and what would you do if they were not true?

CHAPTER

2

WHAT U WORKIN' WITH?

Knowing the weaknesses and strengths of your particular emotional temperament can help you build better relationships and navigate life's circumstances better. Operating blindly can lead us to endless cycles and patterns with unwanted results. The more you know about yourself, the more you're able to craft the life you truly desire.

1. Take the Four Temperaments Test. What is your temperament?

2. What are the strengths of your temperament, and what areas have you seen this positively impact in your life?

3. What are the weaknesses of your temperament, and in what areas in your life have you seen your weaknesses show up?

4. If ignoring our weaknesses leads to repeating negative cycles, then the solution to ending those cycles must be to correct our weaknesses or find a way to turn them into strengths. Pick three of the weaknesses that have impacted your life the most.

5. If you have taken this test before, have you noticed a change in your temperament? If so, what do you think was the cause? Do you feel like your current temperament is representative of your natural state?

CHAPTER

3

I'M EMOTIONAL AND I CAN'T LET GO

Developing an understanding of your emotional makeup, body budget, and how to process your emotions will change how you react, help you destress your life, end toxic relationships, set better boundaries, live from a place of joy, and make better decisions. This will be a big game changer for your life, and the sooner you learn this, the better. Otherwise, you'll spend countless years like me, repeating cycles that you desperately desire to be free from. I've had my fair share of relationships that I should've ended sooner than I did, but because I was afraid of feeling the pain of the separation, I held on too long. If you can identify areas in your life to recognize unhealthy repeating cycles, you're already on the road to transformation.

Developing awareness, cues us into our bodily response and the emotions we are constructing. Read the following scenarios to help you cultivate emotional awareness and identify subjects that might trigger a response.

1. You're video chatting with your siblings, who are all doing really well in their careers and families. They ask you how you're doing, and you've just lost your job and ended things with your boyfriend. Do you tell them the truth or pretend you're doing great. Why? How does that make you feel, and what emotions arise for you? How do those emotions manifest in your body?

2. You've been following friends on social media and you're noticing how good their lives are: finding a great new job, going on beautiful vacations, just getting engaged, purchasing a new house, or announcing they're pregnant. How does that make you feel, and what emotions arise for you? How do those emotions manifest in your body? How do you handle it?

3. You applied for your dream job, but you were just rejected as a candidate. How does that make you feel, and what emotions arise for you? How do those emotions manifest in your body? How do you handle it?

4. You're sitting at lunch with a friend. As you talk, you notice they keep looking at their phone and occasionally pick it up and begin typing, while telling you they're still listening. And you respond _____. How does their treatment of you make you feel, and what emotions arise for you? How do these emotions manifest in your body?

5. Are there cycles in your life that you can identify in the area of money, relationships, family, or health? If so, what is the trigger, what's your emotional response, and what's the end result of the situation?

6. What are some ways that culture has impacted your beliefs, values, communication, expectations, relationships, money, job choice, and health?

7. What are the top three emotional responses you'd like to learn to repurpose, and how do you think it impacts your current state?

CHAPTER

4

SELF-LOVE, SELF-CARE...AF

1. Define what self-care means to you.

2. List your favorite self-care activities.

3. Circle suggested self-care activities.

4. Have you been feeling burned out? In what are some areas you can practice releasing control?

5. If you could create a morning or evening ritual as part of your self-care practice, what activities would you do?

6. Do you love yourself? In what ways do you demonstrate love to yourself and in what areas can you improve?

7. Have you been feeling uneasy, tense, or nervous about someone or something and are feeling uncomfortable about speaking up? What aspects of the situation or relationship are making you feel this way and what boundaries could you create?

CHAPTER

5

IF YOU'RE HAPPY
AND YOU KNOW IT

1. What defense mechanisms do you identify with?

2. What other emotional patterns do you see operating in your life?

3. On a scale from 1-10, 1 being needs improvement and 10 being the most mature, how far along are you on your emotional maturity journey?

CHAPTER

6

SHAME-THE TRIGGER OF ALL MY BUTTONS

1. What's the last experience you had that has brought you shame?

2. What deep-rooted shame issue did the experience trigger, and why?

3. How did your body respond when you were feeling shame?

4. What negative self-talk came up for your during that experience?

5. In what ways could you have shown yourself compassion?

6. Next time you experience an event like this, who can you reach out to share your experience with?

CHAPTER

7

ANGER-DETONATE IN CASE OF THREAT

1. What childhood wounds created the most anger and why?

2. Did your family allow you to express your anger? Why or why not?

3. Was anger regularly expressed by your family. If so, how?

4. If anger was not commonly expressed in your family, how did you learn to handle your anger?

5. When you get angry, what is your physiological response?

6. How do you cope when you're angry?

7. What are some strategies you can employ when you're angry?

_____

_____

_____

_____

CHAPTER

8

UNFORGIVENESS: YOU CAN'T CHANGE HOW I FEEL

1. Who is the number one person I need to forgive right now, and why?

2. What impact has rumination played in perpetuating unforgiveness toward my offender?

3. How has my unresolved anger affected my physical and emotional health, relationships and work?

4. What can I do now to resolve the pain and consequences of how my offender treated me?

5. How can I grieve my sadness and pain and also use it to care for myself?

6. In what ways can forgiveness set me free from unwanted emotional suffering and allow me to have a better relationship with God, myself, and others?

7. What meaning have I discovered through my suffering and forgiveness process?

....

....

....

....

CHAPTER

9

GRIEF-HOW AM I SUPPOSED TO LIVE NOW?

JOURNAL PROMPTS TO PROCESS LOSS

1. I seem to cry most when:

2. The worst thing about my loss is:

3. I give myself intentional space to grieve by:

4. I'm doubling down on self-care by:

5. Guilt or regret seem to come up most when:

6. The most important thing I've learned:

7. For me to find and have balance, I need to:

_____

_____

_____

_____

CHAPTER

10

SETTLING-I THINK I'LL STAY AWHILE

1. Do you see patterns in the type of people that you have dated that may speak to a childhood wound? If so, what are they?

2. What are your personal values?

3. What are your non-negotiable values that need to be present in your partner?

4. What is my purpose?

5. Does my purpose align with this person's purpose?

6. Have you ignored red flags in a partner in the past? If so, how did that impact you?

7. Do you struggle with receiving in a relationship, if so what are some beliefs that you have about giving and receiving that could be blocking you right now?

CHAPTER

11

STRESS-I'M SUPER WOMAN AND I DON'T NEED TO REST

1. What is your pattern when it comes to receiving help?

2. What beliefs do you have around asking for help? Why do you feel that way?

3. What are your main barriers to receiving help (for example, shame or guilt)?

    ....

    ....

    ....

    ....

4. How does your body respond when help or assistance is offered to you?

    ....

    ....

    ....

    ....

5. In what ways can you practice saying yes to help now?

    ....

    ....

    ....

    ....

CHAPTER 12

ANTI-SELF- I WISH I WAS _ _ _ (FILL IN THE BLANK)

THE CRITIC AND THE CHEERLEADER

1. What does your inner critic say to you? Rewrite it from the cheerleader's view.

   Critic:

   Cheerleader:

THE CRITIC AND THE CHEERLEADER

2. What does your inner critic say to you? Rewrite it from the cheer-leader's view.

    Critic:

    Cheerleader:

YOUR WANTED LIST

3. Remind yourself of your wonderful qualities as well as who will value you most.

COURAGEOUS AND CONFIDENT

4. Make a commitment to yourself to do something that scares you a little and requires you to step out in confidence each day. List a week of activities below:

_____

_____

_____

WEEK FOCUS: _____

Mon:	
Tue:	
Wed:	
Thu:	
Fri:	
Sat:	
Sun:	

CHAPTER

13

COMPARISON-IT'S THE PICTURES FOR ME

1. In what areas do I compare myself most to other people?

2. What's motivating you, what in your life do you feel like you need more of?

DESIRES AND ACHIEVEMENTS

3. Make a list of 10 things you desire to have and 10 things you're grateful you already have.

DESIRES

1. ....

2. ....

3. ....

4. ....

5. ....

6. ....

7. ....

8. ....

9. ....

10. ....

ACHIEVEMENTS

1. ....

2. ....

3. ....

4. ....

5. ....

6. ....

7. ....

8. ....

9. ....

10. ....

CHAPTER

14

LONELINESS-BUT
I LOVE MYSELF

1. Is your loneliness experience chronic or situation specific? Why do you feel it is that way?

    ....

    ....

    ....

2. What are your top 10 core values and beliefs?

Values

1. ....

2. ....

3. ....

4. ....

5. ....

6. ....

7. ....

8. ....

9. ....

10. ....

Beliefs

1. ....

2. ....

3. ....

4. ....

5. ....

6. ....

7. ....

8. ....

9. ....

10. ....

3. What do you love doing or talking about that makes you forget about time?

4. What you hate is a clue to something you are assigned to correct. What irks you the most that you wish you could correct (in your environment, city, or society)?

5. What grieves you is something that you were assigned to heal. What makes you sad and moves you to compassion (in your environment, city or society)?

CHAPTER

15

ANXIETY-LET'S GET IT POPPIN'

MY ANXIETY TRIGGERS ARE...

1. List the situations, people, objects or places that tend to trigger your anxiety.

1. ....

2. ....

3. ....

4. ....

5. ....

6. ....

7. ....

2. When you get anxious, what is your body's physiological response?

    ....

    ....

    ....

    ....

3. How do I try to protect myself when I am feeling anxious (avoidance, aggression, alcohol or drug use, compulsive behavior)?

    ....

    ....

    ....

    ....

4. Do you have thoughts that come up continually and make you feel anxious? List them below.

    1. ....

    2. ....

    3. ....

    4. ....

    5. ....

    6. ....

    7. ....

5. Transform your anxious thoughts from above into affirmations and list them below.

    1. ....

    2. ....

3. ....

4. ....

5. ....

6. ....

7. ....

ABOUT THE AUTHOR

Sherese Shy-Holmes is a speaker, coach, and entrepreneur. Known for her ability to shift women from confusion to clarity in just one conversation, she empowers women with practical strategies that generate results. With a formal education in business, taxes, and auditing, Sherese uses a no-fluff approach to formulating ideas, developing an action plan, and creating solutions for her life and business coaching clients. She defines herself as the "Business Doula" that helps ambitious, spiritually-minded women monetize their purpose, navigate solo business development, and break their financial glass ceilings.

She is the founder of Empowered to Prosper, whose mission is to foster a rich growth and support community for women to achieve their life and business goals through workshops, women's circles, courses, and coaching.

Blog: https://www.thebizdoula.com

(Click on "Contact Me" to inquire about having Sherese speak at your event)

Podcast: https://healandsell.buzzsprout.com

Instagram: https://www.instagram.com/thebizdoula

Tik Tok: https://www.tiktok.com/@thebizdoula

Facebook: https://www.facebook.com/thebizdoula

www.ingramcontent.com/pod-product-compliance
Lightning Source LLC
Chambersburg PA
CBHW070453130626
46553CB00006B/2384